Pain Redeemed

{when our deepest sorrows meet God}

ISBN: 978-1480049475
ISBN-13: 1480049476

Pain Redeemed
Published by Natasha Metzler
3837 State Rt. 177
Lowville, NY 13367

Cover design by Natasha Metzler

Personal Study Questions by Brianna Siegrist

Bonus Material
Dying of Thirst
at the Side of a Well
© 2013 Natasha Metzler

Art Work © 2013 Brianna Siegrist

Natasha Metzler

Praise for *Pain Redeemed*

Though I have not faced the pain of infertility, Natasha's eloquent voice echoes my own heart's journey, and reminds and clarifies all God has been trying to teach me. – Trina Holden, author of *Embracing Beauty*

[Natasha] puts her finger on the crux of the matter—not the infertility, not the form of the pain, but overcoming the pain by bringing glory to Him through it all. – Gretchen Louise

Your trial may be different, but the Biblical truths shared in *Pain Redeemed* make it a timeless message. – Carrie

I found encouragement for the journey in this book so full of "wisdom pearls" and hard-won courage. I found new strength and I am grateful for a *Pain Redeemed*. – Lorretta

The story [in *Pain Redeemed*] is engaging, the language is comfortable to read. The message is eternal. – Brianna

Natasha invites her readers along in her journey and reveals how scripture, tears and faith paved her road to contentment. – Susan

Pain Redeemed

Dedicated to

Mama

the bravest woman I know

Introduction

Those days were long and dark. Days that blended into months.

Over and over I found myself in tears. I would lecture my emotions and fight my sorrow but I would still end up beaten and bruised and heartbroken.

Infertility is a silent monster that slowly steals joy until there is nothing left. I can't tell you how long I hid the truth from myself but I know that time passed and I stood empty.

In the book of Isaiah, God says, *Why should you be beaten anymore?...your whole head is injured, your whole heart afflicted. From the sole of your foot to the top of your head there is no soundness—only wounds and welts and open sores, not cleansed or bandaged nor soothed with oil.* (1:5-6)

I was clinging to my bitter pain and God was calling me. He had not forgotten. He was pleading with me, *Why, Tasha, why? Why are you staying in this place of torture? You're wounded. Let me care for you...*

He wanted to cleanse my sorrows. He wanted to bandage my brokenness. He was begging and I was so blind and deaf that I chose to stumble in darkness instead of dancing in light.

God didn't leave me there. He called me out. I still remember the day that I read those verses in Isaiah and realized they were written for me. God, in His graciousness, pulled me up and set my feet on firm ground.

I've been listening to a lot of women. Hurting, broken women. They look alive and well but inside there are wounds and welts and open sores. I hear their stories and see the flicker of pain in their eyes. They live in darkness too.

I know that place. I've lived there. I came out of there. And I still slide back there far too often. I long for us all to find a way to live in the light. The brilliant, life-giving light.

This book is a story about sorrow but it is also about God. It's a story about me but it's also about you.

Your pain may be different than mine. There are hundreds of ways that heartache can rip through our lives. The kind of pain doesn't change the truth. *God is the same no matter what type of agony we face.*

Personal Study Guide

1. What are your reasons for picking up this book? What pain is looming in your life?

2. What do you think of when you hear the word redeemed? What does redemption mean to you?

3. I've shared a picture of a God who cares intimately about the sorrows and pain in our lives.

Have you known God to be like this, or is your image of God more callous, unfeeling, or vindictive?

4. Take a minute to read Isaiah 1:5-6. How do you react? Do you have wounds and sores that need tending?

Chapter One

"They were days of darkness.
Days of crawling and crying
and longing for something to break free.
They were days of me without You.
Dark days indeed."
-from my journals

My story starts in a doctor's office when I was nineteen years old. When the words *strong chance of never bearing a child* were first applied to me. In that place where the mother-heart in me broke and bled sorrow into my life.

I was wounded and desperate. I clung to the babies around me unable to truly believe that I would never taste the gift of a child of my own. Being a mom was in my blood. Half a dozen children had littered my daydreams and now I was being told that I may never have even one.

I struggled through a period of disbelief, but my personality wasn't one to duck and hide. I decided that I could be tough enough to carry this burden. I thought I could continue walking through life—dragging this pain behind me.

I did it for a time. Then a wonderful man asked for my hand in marriage and I saw my hopes of building a family with him burn and crumble into ashes. My feet knocked out from under me and what had been dragging behind snuck up and consumed my life. I couldn't breathe, let alone stand. Any strength I had was lost in the pain.

The trips to the doctor began two months after the wedding. I ducked my head in our small-town waiting room, cringing in silence as I heard people whisper, "I think she's pregnant. I saw her at the doctor's office."

My body was betraying me on every turn. Weight clung to my waist, nausea left me white-knuckled and weak. The doctor told me to lose weight. *Just five percent of your body weight could stimulate ovulation.* I was given this medication and then that one. They left me miserable and unable to lose weight. I was on a diet that cut out nearly everything. *No sugar. No white flour. No meat. No dairy.* I had a constant metallic taste in my mouth that made it hard to drink water. I was angry, hurting, and hopeless.

I married a good man who loved me deeply and made our first year of marriage beautiful in every way he could. But after every moment of joy came the never-ending sorrow. I falsely believed that I could mourn and move on but I soon found that the pain moved with me.

I cried blistering tears over my sister-in-law's ultra-sound pictures and then did it all over again when her next baby came. I held the baby of a teenage mother and burned with jealousy. I took pregnancy tests and stopped looking at the results. Later, I would pull them out of the trash, just to see.

Over and over, I found myself weeping bitterly as hoped-for pregnancies proved to be only wishful thinking.

I felt stupid and foolish.

I felt guilty for my jealousy and tears at someone else's joy. I felt alone and lost and wanted to hide myself in a closet and never face the world again. It was like the word *failure* was tattooed on my forehead.

When the doctor told me, again, that it was my fault I wasn't pregnant that *I simply wasn't trying hard enough* I came home shaking and my husband took one look at my tear-stained face and said, "No more." The medication went into the trash and I disappeared inside myself.

I closed my mouth tight and shrugged my shoulders at friendly questions. I cut myself off from the people best able to help me heal and allowed the weight of every lie I had believed to press me down. I decided that the reason for my inability to get pregnant was simply that I had failed. I should have been able to lose weight or spend more money on a better doctor or give up my desire for children and just be happy.

The problem with darkness is that it blinds you. Things that once brought joy can cause pain in darkness. Tripping over your favorite chair in the middle of the night will leave bruises.

I didn't realize I was walking blind. I had no idea. It seemed like everything was banging against me, leaving welts. I couldn't understand why.

My relationships were in tatters. Why was everyone coming at me with clubs? I grew angry because I couldn't figure it out. I had no idea that all these poor people were just standing there, helpless, while I tripped and fell over them. I was trying to act like I could see and it wasn't working.

My relationship with God was subject to raging moods. I never doubted who He was but I doubted that His plan was good. I looked around and saw only blackness, even when I thought I was staring at His face.

It took one brave person to change the tide. My mother. She showed up at my door, sat me down at the kitchen table, looked me in the eye, and said, "Tasha, you're depressed."

Something inside me snapped. The depression didn't leave but it was identified, labeled. The confusing blackness had a name.

There wasn't much else that changed. I still got bruised. I still felt intense pain. I still cried millions of tears. I was still angry. I still felt completely abandoned and left in a hopeless world where every dream was snatched from my hands. I still couldn't seem to hear or see God. I can't tell you how many of my journal entries included the phrase, "I just want my body to be normal."

But I knew that things were not as they seemed. There was a cloud of depression shrouding my vision and what I thought was real, was actually a lie.

I began crying out God. I let my questions and dreams and sorrows pile at His feet. I filled my journals with prayers for healing and understanding. I wanted to see His face again, no matter what it took.

I didn't recognize it at the time but parts of me were coming back to life.

I started looking for answers to my physical problems and found things that the doctors had overlooked. I searched all over the internet and found that there were dozens of sites that focused on natural fertility help. Naturally Knocked Up (naturallyknockedup.com), Frugal Granola (frugalgranola.com) and Fertility Flower (fertilityflower.com) were all instrumental in teaching me about cycles and herbs and other non-medical techniques in aiding fertility.

I found that the diet the doctor had put me on had literally starved my body for nutrients. Vegetables without good fats and proteins were useless and all of my body's natural defenses were gone. Finally, some of my physical problems began to make sense.

I still felt like something precious had been taken away from me. I spent many nights staring at the ceiling, wishing I could go back to being eighteen years old, healthy and full of dreams. But I was trying.

It was around then that my husband and I were

asked to work for a year at a mission in Haiti. The decision to go filled my heart with peace for the first time in months. I walked on the airplane with a backpack of empty journals, notebooks full of information on natural healing, and a heart that was desperate to be made whole.

Journal Entries

Winter 2008

Do You ever feel like screaming, God?
Because I do on a regular basis.
I want to be whole and strong and beautiful
Instead I am empty, weak and ugly.

Isn't this the story of life? I want to be joyful but I'm so full of sadness and I can't escape it. I want to be whole but I feel so empty. I want to be strong but I wallow in weakness. I want to be beautiful, *Oh, God, how I want to be beautiful,* but I'm ugly with sin and aching pain.

So there You have it. The ugly, nasty me—angry at the perfect, loving You.

Summer 2008

Nothing is quite as painful as watching dreams die. It's like tearing a part of yourself away from your body. An arm, a leg. Maybe ripping a corner of your heart out of your chest.

Sometimes the pain is so deep it feels like you can't breathe.

Sometimes when they are starting to die, life bleeding its way out...the anger is so great that you want to kill them yourself, throw them against a wall, trample them under your feet, and get the dying over with.

This has been the year of dead dreams and sometimes I don't think I can handle any more pain.

Personal Study Guide

1. Where does your story start? When can you look back and say that the struggle you're going through began?

2. How have you tried to ignore, push down, or deny the pain, disappointment, hurts that you were carrying?

3. Was there any way you attempted to "fix" your problem that didn't succeed? How did it contribute to your pain?

4. What labels have you placed on yourself as a result of the struggle? Do you identify with the times that I felt stupid, foolish, and guilty?

5. How has your pain cut you off from others?

6. How has your pain cut you off from the Lord?

7. If you feel you can't hear or see God, if your relationship with the Lord is full of anger and bitterness, are you ready to let yourself come back to life, even if it's painful?

8. Ask the Lord to bring hope back into your life- that you will again have a heart that is whole, that your pain will be redeemed.

Chapter Two

"Lord, I want to see."
-Luke 18:41

I knew my body was overrun with toxins and chemical substances so the first thing I did after arriving in Haiti was a fast. Three days of nothing but water and potassium broth (potato skins, onion, carrot skins and garlic in a pot of water, simmered for about an hour and strained) and then slowly working in whole milk, fruits and vegetables. After that I added in the traditional Haitian diet of rice and beans.

I felt like my body, which been tilted sideways, righted itself. The depression lifted and I seemed to wake up from a long, painful sleep.

As the blindness of physical depression fell away, I was forced to look true at my spiritual state. It wasn't pretty. My beliefs in a loving God had faltered. I felt as if He had abandoned me in my sorrow. My body was correcting itself but my heart still hurt.

I was unsure of how to fix it so I did the only thing I knew. I opened my Bible to Genesis and started reading. *In the beginning God created the heavens and the earth...* (Genesis 1:1)

With every page I cried out, *Jesus, meet me here.*

He's not a god to be commanded at will but He *is* a God who comes to help us in our weakness. A God who lovingly touches the very core of our emptiness.

Page after page, I read and prayed. I kept going and the days began to blend together. I wanted answers but soon I simply hungered for more.

There is something startling that happens when you read the Scriptures all together. Who Jesus truly is fills your vision and the darkness fades. I found that God still makes blind eyes see and deaf ears hear. I know because I was blind and deaf and now I see and hear.

The Old Testament came to life for me. There in the words of the prophets I heard God's desperate plea. I watched the war that battled between His justice and His mercy, and in the midst of it His cry of pain. I caught glimpses of my broken-hearted Savior. One so desperate for the salvation of His people that He was willing to come to earth and take their sins upon Himself.

In Jeremiah, He wavers between saying, *You are unfaithful, you must be destroyed,* and *You are my loved ones. You were made for me! Come back!* As I read through chapter upon chapter I could see why Jeremiah was called the "weeping prophet"; he prophesied the words of a weeping God.

In my mind I could see the King of all kneeling before the blood-stained Israel saying, *Oh, my anguish, my anguish! I writhe in pain. Oh, the agony of my heart! My heart pounds within me; I cannot keep silent.* (Jeremiah 4:19 NLT) *Why? Why have you left me? Why have you done this? Why won't you turn back to me? I have to destroy you but if you would just come back then I could redeem you! I would forgive everything. But you keep going; you keep searching for other gods. Why?*

Yet, even there He promises that He will still save them. At the end of every proclamation of anger and frustration the tone changes and His words soften and a promise to bring them back echoes the name of Jesus through the dripping of His tears.

The mighty nation that God built up from one man falls into a heap. Yet, still, He loves. He saves a remnant. He *always* saves a remnant.

His love song started in the depths of my being as my gaze skimmed through the Minor Prophets. His voice crested and broke over me. *I love you. I chose you. You turned from me. You mocked me. You hated me. You became everything that I can never be. But I love you still. I want you. Return to me.*

As the pages turned to Matthew I felt the relief of the New Covenant after the pressing burden of the Old. I heard Him say, "I have to punish you because I am just but because I love you, *I will bear your punishment.*" I saw again that all the pain on this earth is here because of our rejection of Him and He too has wept at the agony we will face because of it. His mercy was breathtakingly beautiful. His understanding of my pain an incredible, life-altering realization.

Truth settled. Inside every one of us there is a remnant of God's perfect counterpart—the thing we were created to be. God wasn't the one that had turned away. It had been my choice to stop listening, to stop seeing. Just as Eve had rejected God's word as truth, I too had rejected Him. And all the while, He was waiting, *longing,* to gather me to Himself.

Twenty-six days after reading *In the beginning,* I read, *Amen. Come, Lord Jesus.* (Revelation 22:20)

In the quietness I faced my own revelation.

I still struggled with the fact that I knew that God was capable of healing my body and He was choosing not to. So I threw my question at His feet. *Why?*

God said, "What do you think healing looks like to me?"

If I was to stand before God perfectly healed, what would I look like? Not standing before a mirror. Not standing before another person. If I was to stand *before God*, completely healed, what would I see?

Oh, God...I would be whole.

Because if I was whole, I wouldn't be staring down at empty arms, desperate for a child. If I was whole, I wouldn't be depressed. If I was whole, I wouldn't feel like there was a part of me rotting away in death.

No. I would be standing straight with my eyes on Christ, not myself. My heart would be overflowing with joy. My mind would be filled with thoughts of Him.

I finally saw and understood that, to God, healing looks like wholeness.

Journal Entries

2009

I'm coming to understand two things.

1.   I am not in control of my fertility.

We like to think that we control so much. We dictate how many children we have through birth controls so therefore we think that we control how few children we have. With that mindset I have believed that my lack of children is my own fault. Which is why I've been so depressed! *The Word of God says that He is the one who opens and closes wombs.*

2.   Healing, in God's eyes, is wholeness. Not necessarily being perfect physically.

This is, after all, what I long for, right? To be whole.
And for each person it may look different! For some people it may come in the form of miraculous healing. For others in the form of ministry or passion or simply peace.

For me, I don't know yet!

It may be that my body will heal and I will bear the children I desire. It may be that God will give me a ministry and touch lives through my pain. It may be that we will adopt a houseful of children from war-torn Liberia.

The list is endless but there is one thing I know for certain, now. Today. God promises wholeness. **He doesn't leave His children broken and bleeding all over the place.**

He makes us whole.

"Seek me and live." He says. It really is that simple.

Everything in me still screamed with the longing to be a mom. Especially there, in that hot desolate land where, everyday, I had women offering me their children.

In Haiti, so many have babies that they can not care for. A poor year of farming and the people are scraping to feed themselves. Every child is an extra mouth. When a white woman walks into their village, the solution seems simple: give the children to her.

I spent hours one afternoon at the mission hospital holding a set of twins. This little boy and girl were so malnourished that I thought they were less than three months old when they were actually over six. I fed them and washed the sores on their backs. I gave them new clothes and put lotion on their fragile skin.

Every week they came to visit me and the babies would reach for my arms. Every week their parents would say, "You can have them." Every week I would drip tears on freshly washed brown skin and wish with everything in me that the laws in Haiti didn't keep me from adopting.

Depression pressed toward me again.

Physically, I was doing well. Spiritually, I was healing. Emotionally, everything threatened to crumble. I wanted to disappear inside myself. I wanted the questions to stop coming. I wanted, so very desperately, to snatch up those babies and keep them forever, even if it meant not leaving Haiti for ten years so they could be mine.

I felt the old anger toward God building back up. *What is the point of this?*

His voice washed over like a gentle cleansing rain. *The point is that they are my little ones and they have been neglected and need a mother's heart to help heal their bodies.*

But, God, I whispered, *I can't handle this. I feel so lost and alone.*

I was holding the little girl, rubbing my hand down her now-smooth leg as she drank a bottle full of nourishing formula instead of rice and water. God's answer echoed so loudly that I snapped my head up to look around. *That is not truth. I am with you and I'm not lost at all.*

With His voice ebbing and flowing over me I somehow found the strength to keep working and loving and giving. I pushed my sorrows away and clung to His truth. The last time I saw my babies I kissed their pudgy cheeks and sent them off with their daddy and a bag full of soap, lotion and formula.

They had been mine for a season and now they were not. *And I felt peace.*

Personal Study Guide

1. In this chapter, I relate my search for the Lord through the Scripture. What place has the Bible had in your life? Have you been diligently reading and searching through the Bible for him?

2. What toxins have filled your body and mind that the truth needs to clean out and replace? Ask the Lord to open your eyes to see the lies you've been believing.

3. Have you ever read the Bible from cover to cover? If so, what concepts and messages do you think are the foundational threads? If not, what keeps you from doing it?

4. What does it mean when a scripture "comes to life?" Have you had that happen? What do you think makes it happen?

5. I shared that, "God wasn't the one that had turned away. It had been my choice to stop listening, to stop seeing." Is this true in your life? Could it be that he is "even now waiting, longing, to gather you to Himself?" What are the questions you have that keep you from believing that?

6. I listed two things as key:

    -We are not in control of our fertility.
    -Healing, in God's eyes, is wholeness.

How do you react to these two statements? Do you agree? Are these statements encouraging or discouraging? Freeing or Binding?

7. Can you choose to trust the Lord, trust that he has a good plan for you, even if his answers are not your answers?

Chapter Three

"You can fight the fires or accept them,
But the fires will come.
I love you too much to stop them."
-God (from my journals)

After returning home from Haiti, I studied natural healing more in depth. One thing that kept cropping up was the benefits of raw milk. My husband and I prayed and felt led to buy a herd of dairy cows. While we were in Haiti our land had been rented out and the barn closed up. In coming home, our dream was to utilize our farm somehow and this would accomplish that *and* give me access to all the hormone-free raw milk I could use.

It seemed to be the last needed boost that my body required. We had been milking for two months when I ran out behind the barn to throw up my breakfast. Three positive tests later (I didn't believe the first two) I told my husband and sister-in-law.

The fall leaves seemed more beautiful, my husband's smile bigger. I started calculating when a baby conceived in September would be born.

Two days later I woke up to blood.

I was heartbroken. And bitter.

My journals filled with my emptiness and desperation. It had truly never occurred to me that God would allow me to get pregnant and then miscarry. I tried to take it in a stride and once again fell flat on my face.

The crawl up from depression seemed sharper this time. There was less anger at God and more horror at my own failures. But He was there, even then.

Journal Entries

October 13, 2010
For two beautiful days I thought my dreams had come to fulfillment. But death slipped in. I don't feel like I've lost a child, but I do feel like a desperate something from the depths of my heart has been squashed and left to die.

December 2010
~~God, please, please, let me get pregnant again.~~
(I wrote this and then scribbled it out.)

January 1, 2011
Lord, cleanse me this year. There is so much ugliness building and scraping through my life. I want to be filled with You. Only You. Passion for Your Word. Not even

passion against pain or struggles or sin but passion *for You.*

Bitterness. Why am I so bitter, Lord? Where did this come from? How did it sneak up on me and fill my life? God, heal me!

I think I may be crazy. Dumb. Stupid. Idiotic. **Crazy.** I try so hard to be lovely. But I'm not. I'm not anyone's love. I'm nasty. Sin-filled. I DISAPPOINT EVERYONE THAT I LOVE.

I hate it! DID YOU HEAR ME? I. HATE. IT.

Why am I here, Lord? Huh?
To minister to kids? I CAN'T.
To be a wife? I SUCK AT IT.
To be a friend? I'M THE WORST.
To be in a relationship with you? I DON'T KNOW HOW!
All the things that once drew me close to You now seem to mock me.

So now what? There isn't anything left. Not one single thing.

I'm sorry, God. I'm so sorry....

January 2, 2011
Even now, with the morning light streaming through my window, I hurt.

Oh, God, how I hurt.

I can't even feel bad for my crazy rant because I still hurt.

Heal me, O Lord, and I will be healed; save me and I will be saved, for you are the one I praise. (Jeremiah 17:14)

Lord, I know fully, that You can heal. I believe it. I guess I just feel like I can't figure it out. I've always been able to figure out the answers to my trials but this time, I don't like any of my answers. So here I am...

In Scripture you're called **Jehovah-Rapha.** The Lord my Healer. *The One who takes my bitterness and makes it sweet.* Can You be that for me?

I continually turn to myself, but I can do nothing... You alone are the giver of life. You alone have the power to heal.

January 10, 2011
God, I'm so scared. Everything is pointing to another pregnancy and I'm so afraid that in a week I'll be scribbling this out.

Jesus, if I'm just days away from crushed hopes—*please, please, please*—take the bitterness that is sure to come pouring out and *make it sweet.*

January 13, 2011
Time to face the music. Negative. If I could somehow write a scream, I would.

Why, Lord? What was the point of that? And what the heck am I suppose to do now? If there is some way for me to understand, show me. I'm listening!

Oh, Father, the only thing I hear is accusations and sorrow.

"If you had...if you had…"
"Never will you have a baby."
"NEVER, NEVER, NEVER."

I know that isn't you.

Can't You speak louder?!?!

January 15, 2011
Going crazy again. Was folding laundry and caught a glimpse of myself in the mirror. All I could see was fat. Every glaring fault that I have that the doctor said,

"this is why, this is why, this is why..."
"if you had, if you had, if you had..."

And all I could think was **No! NO! NO! I can't do it, God! I can't do this again. I'M DONE.**

Oh, God... my crying heart can't help but ask— if You won't even heal this little thing then how do I know that You'll even save me from my sins? The sins that have been piling up at my door. Threatening to fill my heart and life back up with **DEATH. DEATH. DEATH.**

I know this sounds crazy, but I don't feel perfectly sane anyway.

January 16, 2011
This morning is so quiet. The calm after the storm. I talked to Amos. Put everything away. All the charts and thermometers. All the herbs and supplements. I'm not going to look, think, pray...Not for awhile anyway. Maybe never again.

I just want peace, Lord. Forget about Rapha and the healing, just, *please*, I beg of You, give me peace.

January 26, 2011
Well, Lord, here we are again. Me with all my sin & ugliness—searching for You, Your blood and forgiveness.

I know that You'll hear me. Answer me. Give me peace.
But it doesn't seem like You should.

Still, I'm here. For **You alone have the words of life.**
Pour life back into me, Jesus.

Oh, grave, where is your victory?
Oh, death, where is your sting?

My walk through the miscarriage shook me to my very core. On one hand, I had hope. I *did* get pregnant, even if I hadn't made it past six weeks. It seemed that my body was capable of conceiving.

But I also came to understand the depths of my unbelief. I was scared to ask God for a baby—not because I didn't think He *could* give me one but because I truly did not think that He *would*.

I tried, hard, to put together my thoughts on faith, on God and on this painful journey that He was leading me through, into a blog post.

"On Faith"

Cleaning the milk tank is not my favorite job. The milk-stone (traces of milk that have dried on) can be hard to scrub off.

This morning as I was dipping the long handled brush into hot soapy acid-water and beginning to scrub, I sighed in frustration. My glasses were fogging up. I kept cleaning, waiting for the fog to lift so I could make sure everything was done right. Eventually my vision cleared and the sparkling stainless steel came into view. The acid had done its job whether I could see in the moment or not.

So often there are moments when I can't see. There are moments when all of life fogs right up. When I can't see my hand in front of my face, can't see the chair before it bruises my leg, can't hear God's voice because of the yelling in my ear.

The yelling says things like, *Of course you'll never be a mom. Why would God give you children? You wouldn't be a fit mother. You're lazy and selfish. You're constantly filled with prideful, lustful, angry thoughts. Everyday you bow your knee to idols of all kinds. There is nothing in you worthy of anything.*

And all the air squeezes out of my lungs.

Here's the painful honest truth: the fog is a real thing. And those accusations? **Real.** I *am* all of those things.

But it never fails. The enemy will always try to push things a little too far. He gets confident at my weakness and goes for the object of his fury. His voice echoes: *What can your God do for a worthless sinner like you?*

What can He do? It's not about what He can do but **what He's already done.**

It's true. *I am all of those things.* And that's why I need Jesus, why I need His Spirit, why His blood spilt at Calvary.

I am all of those things and I'm *covered in blood.* I am not judged by them. Whether or not I can ever have children has nothing to do with my own merit. Nothing to do with my own abilities. Nothing to do with anything except that I live in a fallen world.

Proverbs 30:15-16 says:
There are three things- no four!-
that are never satisfied:
The grave,
The barren womb,
The thirsty desert,
The blazing fire.

I have to face reality. If I was to conceive this month and have a child in nine months, would I be satisfied? What if I never had another baby? **Ever.**

I know a woman with one baby who desperately wants more. I know a woman with two children who desperately wants more. I know a woman with *six* who desperately wants more. At what point would it be "enough"?

Another painful, honest truth: *If I'm not okay without a child, I never will be with one.*

If I can't figure out how to stand up to the enemy's attacks now, *today*—then changing my circumstances won't change my sorrow.

God allows fog.

He allows it because He wants to build our faith. He's working and changing- *whether we can see in the moment or not.* He bled and died and rose so we could be free.

It's not enough to just say, "Okay, God, I believe in you. Save me." Doing that might break the chains of the enemy, but we still have to walk out of the dungeon. **We have to live like we're saved.**

Oh, God, build my faith. Build and build and build. I want to be solid. Not tossed to and fro by lies from the enemy.

Personal Study Guide

1. I start this chapter with a new location, a new chapter in life, a new plan. How have you tried to "start again" or try something new to change your circumstances? Have you found yourself, as I did, still in the same battle?

2. In my diary entries, we see that I was desperately trying to hold onto the truth while still feeling the pain and discouragement. It might be tempting to think that our roller coaster of feelings make us unqualified for the title "faithful." But refusing to turn away from God, and instead, turning TO him with questions, hurts, and even anger is the only way to be continue a walk with him. Do you "give up" your relationship with the Lord when you have questions or hurts? Or do you press in further?

3. I asked the Lord, "If you won't even heal this little thing, then how do I know that You'll even save me from my sins?" Why does the issue of healing create such a crisis of faith within ourselves? Have you ever come out on the other side of this question? What are your thoughts?

4. Read John 6:60-68. The disciples were struggling with a hard message. What did Jesus ask Peter in verse 67? And how does Peter's response in verse 68 compare with your response? Are you resolved to keep following the Lord? Or do you believe there are other places for answers if His answers are too hard?

5. In the blog post titled "On Faith," I compare the accusations of the enemy to fog that blinds us. What accusations have been filling up your vision? Have you tried to dispel the fog by denying them? Or are you ready to own up to your own failings, weaknesses, and sins, and let the blood of Christ do the work for you?

Chapter Four

In my surrender I will find—
true victory is found in my defeat.
- journal entry

I began feeling a burning need to share about our infertility with those around us. I didn't want to. Not even one little tiny bit.

For some reason, infertility seemed so personal. The thought of opening my mouth and saying, *Hey, guys, we can't have a baby,* seemed like an insurmountable challenge. Sure, a few people knew but they were ones who loved me and knew my heart. Not the general public.

I convinced myself that most people didn't really want to know. Not truly. They asked questions to be nosy, but they wouldn't actually know what to do with my pain.

Learning to humble myself enough to share that I was falling apart was one of the hardest lessons I've ever faced. It became horribly clear that pretending to stand when I was crumbling was actually pride in action. Pride that had a death-grip on my heart.

I was beginning to understand that God did not see me as a failure; however, it was easy to imagine that other people did. The thoughtless comments about weight loss added to the less-than-helpful questions about when we would start our family caused me to build walls and allow pride to dictate my actions.

God did not give up on me. He slowly, steadily, broke down the walls piece by piece.

Mankind was created to interact. When one of us falls down under crushing weight—it is time for the rest to step in. But they have to know the need. They have to hear the pain. They have to see the tears. And that means that I have to speak.

Slowly, I began whispering the truth and I was astounded at what I found. In vulnerability there is true fulfillment. I was right that some people didn't really want to know, but if my vulnerability taught them to be more careful with the next person, was that not worth the painful humbling of my heart?

And the rest of them? The ones who truly longed to reach out and touch me in my heartache? My eyes were open to them.

The lie from the enemy that I was "all alone" had been eating away at my insides. It's his favorite lie to tell. I've seen it repeated in countless forms and every time it is just as hideous, just as deadly.

If you believe you're all alone no one can empathize with you and no one can help you pick up the broken pieces of your life. If you believe you're all alone no one can call you to account for your sin because "they don't understand your pain." And if you believe you're all alone, dear friends, *no one can give you grace.*

It's a hopeless existence and the only way to fight it is to be humble and brave enough to speak.

I have a friend who faced a horrendous tragedy, the birth of a stillborn son. It was heart-shattering.

Death isolates. It leaves people feeling empty, lost, and so very alone. Rachel was no different. Week after week she sat in my Sunday school class saying, "I don't want to be here but I am." Week after week she had to fight the lie of being alone with everything in her. She had to choose to say, "I am *not* all alone", even when it felt like she was.

Then the day came when she whispered, "I know I should be over this by now..." And because she was there and fought the lie, even when it felt like truth, she sat in a room full of women who "didn't know" her pain and grace poured over her.

You just buried a baby, someone whispered in return, *I don't think you need to "get over it".* We hurt with her and cried with her and tasted grace together.

When she gave birth to her next child and told the story of him crying as he was born and of nothing sounding so beautiful—of the nurses and doctors and her husband all crying and how she couldn't shed a tear because all she could think was *he's alive!*—everything in me danced.

And that girl who has never tasted infertility and this girl who has never buried a baby—together we're not alone. When I reach out from my pain to offer her comfort in hers and when she looks up from hers to comfort me—Satan's lies are buried in an avalanche of truth and none of us are really alone.

The lie of being alone is only the beginning. It is followed by more lies and darkness that threatens to keep us buried in sorrow.

The idea that my pain sets me apart from the rest of society is another isolation trick by the enemy. My pain is real, but it is not the only pain. Every single person walking in this fallen world will experience pain. I need to keep my eyes wide open, even through tears, and look for places to offer comfort and love to those around me. I've tasted pain so I now have the privilege of offering empathy to others.

It's okay to identify my pain, to cry buckets of tears about it, to fall apart in desperation. The problem doesn't come until I become so consumed by it that I fail to see the pain around me.

In opening my heart to see and empathize with other's pain, I open my life to His grace. In speaking comfort, I am comforted. In offering empathy, I receive love. In journeying through pain with a friend, I no longer journey alone.

There is no strength, no hope in comparing pain. My pain of infertility cannot be compared to my friend's pain of watching her marriage dissolve. They are different, we are different, but in binding ourselves together we are the same.

Alone we'll slice each other to pieces.

The mother of five, who spent months in the hospital with her youngest child, does not need her ability to have children compared to my lack of ability. We need to bind ourselves together, acknowledging that we both experience pain. She needs me and I need her and together we'll walk through hardships.

My friend who buried a son does not need me to be jealous of the baby she now has. She needs me to rejoice over the son she holds and continue to mourn with her for the son who never took his first breath.

The mom of eight who buried a set of twins needs comfort and compassion, not rationalization that she has other children to be thankful for.

Our pain can refine us or make us bitter. We can look at the world with deeper grace or we can build walls. I can become lost in myself, or give up and lose myself in Him.

Pain, in reality, can bring me the deepest joy if I allow it to do its refining work in my heart. If I allow my pain to tear down walls rather than build them, I will come to find that my relationships are a place of healing wounds rather than a place of being sliced wide open.

In turning my eyes to other's pain, I open myself to see God working.

When I abandon the foolish idea that I'm the only one writhing in sorrow I get the privilege of watching and rejoicing in more victories than just my own.

When the six month old baby of a friend comes out of open-heart surgery and is growing and breathing and learning to roll around and eat her toes, I can laugh and delight in a God who works miracles.

When a marriage that is falling apart with no hope is pulled from the brink by a loving God who redeems brokenness, I can sing praises to a God who works miracles.

When I look around and see hurting lost people, I can offer worship to a God who *knows and understands pain.*

"Moments That Should Never Be"

Yesterday I spent part of my day helping at a private funeral for an infant. With only three weeks left in her pregnancy, a friend of mine was induced so she could deliver her stillborn son.

From the moment I heard the news until even now, my mind kept saying, "No. No. It's not supposed to happen that way." Mamas should never have to bury babies. Dads should never have to watch their legacy be laid to rest. That's just not how it works.

But it happens, all the time. Children die.

Babies die.

Our brilliant hope for the future crumbles into a pile of broken dreams.

I wish, no, I *long* for some way to explain things. Some secret hidden key to unlock the horror of situations like this. A Bible verse. A principle of discipleship. Something. Some way to prove that God has a "happy" thing to counter this depth of sadness.

But guess what? There's not.

We don't have a God who says, in the middle of horrible pain, *I did this because...* There is no explanation. It's not because someone was good or bad or deserved it or didn't deserve it.

It just is.

And there is no "happy" thing to fix it. Not another child. Not another dream. Nothing actually replaces what is lost. Everyone else might forget about that little plot with the marker that has the same date of birth and death... but they won't. Whenever they say the number of children they have this one will always be there, even if they don't speak it.

Yet, even in the middle of that raw grating pain, we do have a God. One who does speak. No, it's not an explanation.

He says, *"I know."*

I have never lived through a death like this one but I have experienced my own tastes of death. I've looked at the horrible and haven't known what to do. I've raged and ranted and screamed at God, asking why or why not, and then crumbled into a heap at His feet, longing for an explanation... and I've felt His tears and I've heard His voice.

The truth is, in the middle of pain the most healing thing to hear is that God knows. And while I may be angry that He didn't protect me or them or whoever, I also have the knowledge that He didn't protect Himself either. My ideal may be protection from pain but God can't actually be molded into my ideal. He is what He is. When Moses asked God who to say had sent him, God said, *I AM*.

He hasn't changed since then.

And for some reason, this God who IS, the One who created us and loves us, is not afraid of pain. He faces it and He lets us face it.

So those moments that should never be...are.

They were for Adam and Eve, for Abraham, for Job, for David, for every generation since and even for God Himself. It makes sense that I will face them and my friends will face them.

Still, it hurts.

So I will cling to the truth. The only truth I have. That my God, the One who IS, the One who created us all, who loves us all...knows.

Have you noticed that pain transcends differences? When my whispers of infertility leaked in my church circles, people stopped. The sound of my hope has filtered in because I feel pain.

It is the same for everyone. I've watched this phenomenon over and over.

DeWitt and Nicole attend my church. I knew them but our lives didn't intersect much until after their fourth child was born. They named her Eden.

She was born with three holes in her heart and pronounced blind and deaf. There were chromosome issues that still haven't been diagnosed. She had to be fed through a stomach tube and the first ten months of her life were spent in and out of intensive care.

Their lives turned upside down. Fear crawled the walls of their home. Would the baby live? Would they be able to communicate with her if she did? But out of their pain rose an aching hope. So loud, so brilliant, it could fill a cathedral. From their darkest moments redemption rang clear.

Nicole spent an afternoon with me, telling me the story of Eden. "We had no idea that there was anything wrong until after the birth," she told me. As the diagnosis came back, piece by piece, they were forced to face reality.

"It became increasingly clear," she said, "that I had to decide if I was going to trust God or not."

They have chosen to trust. To allow their pain to be used for God's glory. To praise Him from the middle of hardship.

It didn't have to be this way. They didn't have to be testimonies of Jesus. They could have crumbled into bitterness. Eden's physical issues may continue to interrupt their lives forever. It's a big deal. They could have clung tight to their heartache and said, "Why me?"

Of course, then they would have missed the miracles.

DeWitt, sitting in his Sunday school class, saying, "I could have lost my wife and daughter but God saved them both." In complete awe and thankfulness.

Nicole, dripping tears and whispering, "They did a new hearing test and she passed it. She isn't deaf."

The beats of joy that radiate when I ask her about Eden's eyesight. "They said she would be blind but watch," her fingers move in front of the baby and the infant follows and tiny hands reach up without hesitation to grab onto her Mama.

The shuddering of miracles that have the power to leave us breathless with hope.

"This has taught me what trust really is," Nicole explained, "I can't control the future, I can only believe that today, God will give me what I need."

Some days are difficult and there are more hard days coming. There will always be questions about tomorrow. Trust is believing that God is here today. Right now. Giving us what we need to survive this moment.

To trust simply means recognizing that there are miracles and there are sorrows and *God is good.*

Personal Study Guide

1. In this chapter, I make a case for sharing our sorrows and personal struggles. Have you been able to do this, or have you been tempted to retreat, and bear it alone? What are the pros and cons of being open about your struggles? Which is the less selfish choice?

2. I shared that, "It became horribly clear that pretending to stand when I was crumbling was actually pride in action." What do you think about this statement? What do you fear will happen if others know your failings, fears, or weaknesses?

3. Have you been tempted to believe you are all alone? Who is in your life with pain that you could encourage and relate to? Ask the Lord to show you a sister who is hurting, even if it is about something completely unrelated to your pain.

4. How have you been tempted to compare your pain to others? To quantify or measure the need you or others have? Have you been tempted to be bitter over the comfort and help others have received while you were hurting? Don't spend time rehashing what you feel is injustice. Instead, what are some ways you can show God that you trust him by giving when you'd like to be getting?

5. What does it mean that we have a God who "knows and understands pain?"

6. Why does it sound so comforting to get an explanation for something? Why does it seem that the answer to the "Why?" question would be enough? Where do you go when there is no answer? How has that affected what you believe about God?

7. When Nicole tells the story of her daughter's health issues, she says, "It became increasingly clear... that I had to decide if I was going to trust God or not." Has this been clear to you? What have you decided?

Chapter Five

*Pain is the fire that refines and burns away
the temporary and the fake,
leaving only what is true and deep."
-journal entry*

Sometimes life is so full of pain that all you can do is breath in and out.

I have spent days in tears. I have escaped to a place where no one can see or hear me and have screamed in agony. I know that my body doesn't work right. I know that I may never have the children my heart desires. I know that I may have to watch my dreams die slowly over a period of time.

Sometimes knowledge hurts.

Mourning is an intricate part of the journey. There is no skipping it, ignoring it, or wishing it away. The only thing to do is to stumble through it. In the process, we will be changed. There is no getting around that either.

One day as I was fighting for breath under the weight of my sorrow, my husband said, "Honey, I'm sorry you hurt but I love who you are because of the hurt."

The words stunned me. Made me lift my gaze from myself. He loved who I was, but I didn't like what I was on the verge of becoming. It became excruciatingly clear that I had a choice as to what I would do with my deepest heartache. I could be refined or I could grow self-consumed and bitter.

There is freedom in mourning as long as we are surrendering ourselves to be changed into the image of Christ in the process. He wants to use our sorrow to heal us, to make us whole. Unfortunately, my sinful tendency is to allow sorrow to turn me away from Him.

My sins need to be carried to the cross of Christ. I need to open the Word of God and devour His words of comfort. In Him I will find the strength to face pain. I will learn the art of allowing Him to transform me *through my pain* so I can offer grace to those around me.

I can desire holiness but to truly attain it, I have to learn the grace of living right here. Even when right here contains pain. I have to learn to love from this spot, today. I have to learn to trust even when His will seems frightening or untrustworthy. I have to follow Him even when it feels like I am walking into emptiness. It is right here, right today, that I must decide where my faith is. If serving God does not work from here, in the middle of my pain and mourning, it won't work from anywhere.

"The Valley of Achor"

The other day I heard some news that left me breathless. Friends told us about the upcoming adoption of their fourth son. Jealousy tore at my insides. Real, sinful, hateful jealousy.

I could pretend it wasn't so but it wouldn't be truth. The truth is that I couldn't help but rail, *"Seriously, God?"* It wasn't a question. It was a scream of protest.

After the tears scalded cheeks and I wallowed in pain for a while, the healed, redeemed part of me took a shaking breath and overcame my flesh. *Okay, God, teach me,* I whispered into the night as I gripped my husband's hand while he slept beside me.

There had been so many glimpses of healing but it seemed that the fullness of it stayed just out of my grasp.

Lifting my face upward, watching the shadows of the moon paint pictures on the ceiling, I said, *I can't stay in this place forever, wallowing in pain whenever someone gets what I long for. Help me. Heal this in me.*

I drifted off to sleep in silence.

As a teenager I had lived in easy joy. From the ages of thirteen to eighteen I bore very little in terms of sorrow and was relentless in my pursuit of God. I found the heart of the God I longed to follow. Zephaniah says, *The Lord your God is with you, he is mighty to save. He will take great delight in you, he will quiet you with his love, he will rejoice over you with singing.* (3:17) and I felt that pouring-out of love from Him. I felt His power and His delight. I heard His song.

Then it all changed.

The feelings faded as life brought twists and turns. My infertility was simply the last of a pile of trouble that seemed to plague me, pressing me down, keeping me from hearing the voice of God. I knew He still loved me. I never doubted His power. Yet, I couldn't come to terms with His silence in the middle of my pain.

The morning after my tears, I slipped away and opened my Bible. The pages crinkled as I turned them and I reveled in the calming effect the noise had on me. This was the Word of God. Everything else may have changed. Life could go completely out of control. I might never be a mother, never be a good enough friend or wife or person, but God's Word was perfect and unchanging.

Therefore I am now going to allure her; I will lead her into the desert and speak tenderly to her. (Hosea 2:14) My gaze skimmed the verse and it felt like life-giving air poured over me. God was not unaware of my desert wanderings. He had brought me here—not to abandon me but to speak tenderly to me.

There I will give her back her vineyards and make the Valley of Achor a door of hope. There she will sing as in the days of her youth, as in the day she came up out of Egypt. (Hosea 2:15) As I eagerly read and reread the words, along with the notes at the bottom of the page, I felt unrelenting joy pour through me. "Achor" means trouble. This valley of trouble, the painful journey of the past few years, the silence of God, this life desert that left me dying of thirst was not the final chapter.

The chain of sorrow that had bound my heart so tightly seemed to snap in two. He promised to make my valley of trouble into a door of hope. He stood there saying, *I will take the sorrow you endure and will create beauty from it. That is, after all, my child, what I do. I make beauty from ashes.*

Scripture is our most effective resource while wading through sorrow. The process of mourning empties us and when we offer our hollow hearts to God, we give Him the right to fill us with true things.

In John 6:41, Jesus is referred to as the *bread that came down from heaven* in a reference to the manna that the Israelites ate in the desert. Every morning it came and it was just enough for that day.

I like to have things lined up and set. Plans made. Life figured out. Infertility stole that ability from me. Every time that I break down and say, *I can't have the babies I want,* in a way, I'm admitting that I am not in control. I'm acknowledging that it is impossible for me to survive even today.

I need Him. *Oh, how desperately I need Him.* Jesus is my manna, my bread. I have to eat and drink what He offers today or I will starve. I can beg, I can plead, I can grow angry, but I am completely dependent on what He gives. And when I grasp and grab for something different—for something more—it is to turn my back on God himself.

He has given so much. I haven't even begun to taste the bounty that He has offered. How many times have I turned my back to Him, stared at what I don't have, and cried that He has abandoned me? *Oh, God, forgive this sinner.*

The beginning, the first step, is to eat of His Word. As truth fills up our emptiness, we learn to acknowledge Him and we are made whole.

"Acknowledgment"

My journal is changing as I'm learning and growing. My Bible is once again staying open on my living room couch so that I can drink of the Living Water through out my day. I feel like I cannot drink enough. And I love this feeling of thirst. Like God is close and I can touch Him and feel Him and know Him and be filled to overflowing. My hands raise to feel the love of the Father rushing down...

Deep calls to deep
In the roar of your waterfalls
All your waves and breakers
Have swept over me... (Psalm 42:7)

Last week's Sunday School lesson on Proverbs 3 has been rolling through my mind. The verse I knew so well. One of hundreds memorized. *Trust in the Lord with all your heart and lean not on your own understanding; in all your ways acknowledge him, and he will direct your paths.* (Proverbs 3:5-6)

One day it stuck out. *Acknowledge Him.* Isn't that what I have been doing as I fill my journal with lists of blessings? Looking at my life, the good, the bad, the painful, the scary, the beautiful, the glorious... and acknowledging Christ in each part?

Baby calves that look like deer fawns
canned peaches filling shelves
fresh apples picked and eaten in fields
my husband's name on my caller ID
nights of no sleep—for they remind me of my
weaknesses and my need for His strength
twinkle lights in evening shadows
rainbows at weddings
community.

God in and around and through. *I sing for joy at the work of your hands.* (Psalm 92:4)

My mind fills with the stories from Sunday. The baby with three holes in her heart. The little girl with a blood disease. The husband with a possibility of prostate cancer. The mother mourning her buried son. The wife facing another season of chemotherapy.

And then me, with all my own fears and hurts and sorrows. The fact that it was one year ago that I was pregnant. And in a month it will be one year since I miscarried.

Acknowledge Him, even in pain. God is the one who created the little girl with holes in her heart. God is the one who understands the complicated diagnoses of blood disease. It is God who has power over cancer and the outcome is His will. God, who took that little boy home before he had really even lived. And it is God who knew that I would never carry that baby for more than six weeks. And He is okay with it. In fact, He has plans and purposes in it.

And my job is not to understand it (lean *not* on your own understanding) but to acknowledge Him in it. To recognize that He is God. Not me. Never me. Never the idols that I create in life. *Only Him.* The One who says:

I have loved you with an everlasting love…
(Jeremiah 31:3)
Do not fear, I will help you…(Isaiah 41:13)
For I will pour water on the thirsty…(Isaiah 44:3)
I long to redeem them…(Hosea 7:13)
Behold, I am making all things new…(Revelation 21:5)

Acknowledge that this world is just a moment. A breath. A blink. And pain may last for the night, but the living truth is that joy comes in the morning.

Personal Study Guide

1. At one point I said, "I had a choice as to what I would do with my deepest heartache. I could be refined or I could grow self-consumed and bitter." How has your pain changed you? How could you submit to the refining process?

2. It might be tempting to believe, "If _____ would be fixed, I would be more _____ (patient, loving, gentle, etc)." Yet, I shared, "If serving God does not work from here, in the middle of my pain and mourning, it won't work from anywhere." How have you been tempted to fill in those blanks? How does my statement refute that?

3. What promises and hopes have you been excited about in the past that have seemed to die off? Ask the Lord to show you his vision for your future.

4. Have you ever been at the place where the Bible is such a source of life to you that you'd like to leave it "open on your living room couch?" Do you have a thirst for the words of the Lord? To touch and feel and know him? Read Psalm 42 and ask the Lord to give you that thirst.

5. In Proverbs 3:5-6, the writer encourages us to "acknowledge him" in all of our paths. How have you applied this in your life, and how can you do that in the future?

Chapter Six

Create in me a clean heart, O God,
And renew a right spirit within me…
-Psalm 51:10 ESV

The day was hot and sultry. A summer afternoon where everything seemed limp and tired. I was dressed in jeans and a purple tank-top, my hair hanging in curls that I kept lifting to allow a little breeze on my neck.

I arrived at the park a few minutes late and walked quietly up to the group. I could see the cake and the crepe paper decorations that hung from the rafters of the pavilion. I set my gift down on the pile and slipped onto a bench beside the only two people I knew.

She was talking and laughing a little. Her hair slung back in a pony-tail, a pink and green graphic-tee stretched over her pregnant belly. She was still a teenager. So was he.

My gift was simple. There were diapers and wipes, a couple outfits and a note that said I was praying for her and the baby—that they would do well and know that they are loved by a God who sees.

I felt like a hypocrite.

All the way there I had battled God with anger simmering. I wanted to be loving but my mind was screaming, *God?! She gets a baby and I live with infertility? She picks out maternity clothes while I just gain weight? She decorates a bedroom while I cry over newborn outfits? The Bible says children are a reward. Want to share with me how that works out? Is she rewarded for living in sin? I probably could have gotten pregnant at seventeen too, you know.*

I hope, *I pray*, that my actions were gentle and loving but my war was far from over.

"I just don't understand you, God," I said aloud once I was safe in my car on the way home, "I know her lifestyle. It's not pretty. Why does she get a baby and not me? I know that I would be a better mom than she will be."

I cringed the moment the words left my mouth. I suddenly pictured myself sitting on the sidelines of a race with a broken leg and watching a girl come limping past. In bitter anger I cry out, "I am a *way* better walker than her! She should have the broken leg, not me!"

Horror filled me and my heart clenched. His presence was so close, so overwhelming, and His words deafening.

Natasha, you alone will stand before me. Not you and her. Not you and anyone else. You alone.

My bitter, foolish, prideful thoughts were showing the ugliness of my heart and I was petrified. I stopped the car beside a little cemetery and walked for some time amidst the tombstones. In defeat, I fell to my knees and begged God for forgiveness.

Oh, God, I am a broken busted-up sinner.

I tried desperately to tear the darkness from my heart. It felt like Eustace in *The Voyage of the Dawn Treader*. He turns into a dragon because of his selfish, greedy heart and in desperation he tries to tear away his skin to clean himself of filth. Layer after layer of scales come off but he is still a dragon.

I knew that I could tear layer after layer of darkness from myself but it would never clean me up. I was empty of the strength to free myself from filth.

In the story, Aslan shows up. In my life, God showed up.

His words began filling the empty places in me. *Children are a reward from me but why does anyone deserve a reward? Your righteousness, child, is like filthy rags compared to My holiness. It is by grace, everything, is by My grace. What have you done to deserve any of the rewards that I have given you? You're looking at this through sin-filled eyes and trying to qualify my love with gifts.*

Truth hit me between the eyes. None of us deserve anything. My mind said that my inability to get pregnant was like a negative God's-favor-test. I wanted to be able to work hard enough to get the things I desired, but that's not how it works.

In the Old Testament, we read of people who served gods of all kinds, idols made of wood and stone. Men believed that if they did the right things, the gods would give them what they desired. They would offer sacrifices to win favors from their deity of choice and go to great lengths to fulfill the commands to get the things they wanted.

Our God is not like other gods. He is not an idol. He is living. Breathing. Moving.

Even during those ancient times before Jesus died on Calvary, when the Israelite people were required to bring sacrifices to the temple, they were not offered to earn favors. Sacrifices were given in thanksgiving or to ask for forgiveness from sins.

When I expect that my "goodness" will win me favors from God, I reduce His awesome holiness to that of a worthless idol.

Oh, God, forgive this sinner.

We're called to make our lives a living sacrifice. To offer a gift that is holy and pleasing to our God. But it is not for earthly rewards. *It is not to win money or popularity or health or even a baby.* I'll put it bluntly: It's not about us.

We're to fix our gaze on Jesus, the author and finisher of our faith.

Pascal, a scientist and theologian from the sixteen hundreds, once referred to human-kind as "licking the earth," in other words, loving earthly pleasures more than God. This terminology brings quickly into focus the depths of our unworthiness. We are dust. We plant our faces into the dirt when God is opening windows into heaven.

At the same time, acknowledging our sin is not so we can live in a state of self-loathing.

Acknowledging that you're licking the earth is not so you can bemoan the taste of dirt.

The acknowledgment of our unworthiness is so we can live in a state of gratefulness as we lift our heads to Him.

God is gracious. He heals. He turns bitter to sweet. But we have to repent. We have to ask forgiveness. We have to see our sin and get rid of it before it consumes us.

That day on the road I came face-to-face with a Holy God and with the knowledge that I am a child of dust. It was a sacred God-moment when I stared at truth and felt my heart transform.

My view, so often, gets distorted. I fail to see the gifts He has given me when I am lusting for more. Children are good and beautiful gifts but so often I elevate them over God in my life. I long for a baby more than I hunger and thirst for Jesus.

It has happened since and I'm sure will happen again, but I cling to the cross that redeems my brokenness. I cling to Jesus. And I learn to accept the rewards He has given me without lamenting or whining (or growing angry and bitter) about the ones He hasn't.

"Ignoring Death"

The first calf that died in our barn was named Grace. She was a pretty little black thing with a white heart on her forehead. When she got sick I sat in the barn for hours trying to coax fluid and medication into her.

I fed her one morning with a bottle because she wasn't strong enough for a bucket. That afternoon I came back and lifted her head to see if she was okay. I dropped her and screamed. Her tongue was hanging out and her eyes open wide in a death-stare. It freaked me right out. I couldn't sleep that night, the horror-story quality of that dead calf burned in my memory.

This morning there were two dead calves. A mama stepped on her new baby and another hung herself by her neck chain. My husband was busy feeding cows so I lugged them into the center aisle and tossed them in a pile for him to take out later and bury.

All during milking I stepped over those dead calves but they didn't bother me much. I mean, I dislike dead animals, but it happens. I didn't look at them, certainly not at their face and unseeing eyes. In fact, I've gotten pretty good at ignoring dead things altogether. They're just there.

In life, the first time I committed a new sin it would freak me right out. The lie that dripped from my lips? *I threw up later that night.* The candy-bar I stole? *I never ate it. It made me ill to look at it.* The first time I harbored a grudge? *I couldn't sleep at night.* The list is endless.

But as the years went by I got better at overlooking my sins. Something in me hardened and I learned to step over and not look death in the face. I learned to ignore and pretend and I got more brazen and my sins ran deeper. Now, sometimes before I know it, my life starts stinking of death.

I tore apart a piece of bread this morning. Just a roll that I was going to slather with butter and jam. And something in me awakened. His voice echoing, *While they were eating, Jesus took bread, and when he had given thanks, he broke it and gave it to his disciples, saying, "Take and eat; this is my body."* (Matt. 26:26)

Why is the cross at the very center of our faith? Why does communion, baptism, being a servant, all of the Christian faith center on death? Because if you don't look death in the face you'll learn to overlook it.

It's what we do!

I walk through life and step over death and ignore it and think that I'm free from it but its still there and I'm still covered in the stench. And God says, *No! Look death in the face. You think it's the face of fear and condemnation? Look again. I conquered death so now I rule it. Look death in the face so you can see Me.*

When we look at death, all the sins that pile up and reek, it loses its power. Because in the face of death, for the believer, is the face of our Jesus. The One who stands between us and condemnation.

The wages of sin is death but the gift of God is eternal life in Christ Jesus our Lord. (Romans 6:23)

When light shines, darkness flees. When truth illuminates, lies cower. When God speaks, the Enemy is silenced.

Therefore, there is now no condemnation for those who are in Christ Jesus, because through Christ Jesus the law of the Spirit of life set me free from the law of sin and death. (Romans 8:1-2)

When I acknowledge my sin, I am freed from it.
Oh, Jesus, thank you, thank you, thank you.

Personal Study Guide

1. Read Psalm 51. Note the author, and the circumstance, listed at the beginning of the psalm. Are you, like David, feeling that your sins are always before you? Or do you feel pretty comfortable that you are mostly free of sins to be cleansed? Read the Psalm again, and ask the Lord to reveal how broken and contrite you are, and whether there are sins that you're overlooking that he'd like to clear away.

2. In this chapter I referenced Psalm 127:3, "Sons are a heritage from the LORD, children a reward from him." In fact, I used this verse while "building a case" for my anger at the situation, and at the Lord. What verses or ideas have you used to build a case against the Lord for what you think is wrong? Ask the Lord to bring them all to mind, and make a list to be used on question 4.

3. I shared some messages in first person that I believe the Lord was saying to me. How do you react to this technique of giving God a "voice?" Is it something you've encountered before? How do these lines that I wrote from him line up or not line up with the messages you've received from him? Does my God look or sound differently to you than the God you've been reaching out to? Do you even believe that God does answer in a "still small voice" anymore? If you do, and you've never identified his voice, take a minute to sit quietly, asking him to speak to you. His voice often sounds like a spontaneous thought that reminds of scripture or truth that you've learned before. He is encouraging, but convicting, and always gentle. Write down what you hear.

4. When I went to the Lord with my diatribe after the shower, I was expecting to be justified in my anger and proof of injustice. But I was horrified to find that I was convicted by my own words of attitudes, beliefs, and thoughts that were sinful. Instead of being comforted, the Lord's words were gently chiding. When you take your thoughts and hurts to the Lord, he is gentle but not coddling. If you really want your questions answered, and for your heart to be clean, you can take your list of grievances to the Lord. But be prepared, they might be a list of evidence that your heart is the one that needs to be broken and contrite. If you are ready, read Psalm 51, and then ask the Lord to reveal the truth about each item on your list.

5. In the blog post "Ignoring Death," I painted a picture of sins in our lives, once startling and ugly, becoming commonplace and unnoticed. What things in your life come to mind when you read this entry? Are there things that you've given up on every being freed from? Read Galatians 6:7-9, and Philippians 1:6. What is the truth in these verses about the things in your life that you've become discouraged about?

6. When was the last time you took time to meditate and focus on the death of your Savior? Do you avoid the gore of the story, and skip on to the resurrection? How is your relationship with the cross like your relationship with your sins? Take time today to look them both right in the face.

Chapter Seven

*"God isn't just concerned about the destination.
He's interested in the journey as well."*
-Delite Lago

I hear it quite a bit. *Don't give up hope...
You're still young... Women have babies in their
forties these days. Lots of time left! God still does
miracles!* In response I usually whisper, *Hopefully.*

How do I explain that there is still sorrow, even
in miracles?

The blind man that Jesus healed in John 9 went
and told everyone he saw about Jesus. He stood
before judges and priests with his testimony. It was
wonderful and beautiful. There was purpose to his
years in darkness. Jesus said, *this happened so the
work of God might be displayed in his life.* (9:3) He
was probably thankful that he had been born blind
so he could taste the touch of the Savior but that

does not mean that his years of blindness disappeared. It simply means that they were not wasted.

I will always mourn the children that will never be. That does not mean that I'll be angry or lack joy, it means that I live in a fallen world and some dreams must die.

Journal Entries

20//

All dreams are not meant to live.
Some exist to die.
And it's okay!
God does good things with dead dreams.
But, oh, how it hurts.

My husband and I went on a four-wheeler ride one evening. We came to a stop overlooking our largest field and watched the sunset. His thirty-seventh birthday had come and gone, and as the last of the rays dipped beyond the windmills, he said, "It really hit me today that I will never have a son of my youth."

The verse from Psalm 127 dripped through our conversation. *Like arrows in the hand of a warrior are the sons of one's youth.* (Psalm 127:4 ESV)
This gift would never be ours and the realization was sorrowful—the burning of a dream. It wasn't angry or bad. It simply was. We both knew that

time never goes backward, even if I conceived that day.

Death is a part of life in a fallen world and dream-deaths have to be mourned with all the rest. We can't stifle the mourning or become consumed with it.

Taking time to say goodbye to one dream does not mean spiraling into hopelessness.

Acknowledging that we will never be young parents does not mean that we have lost all hope of ever being parents.

There are times to clean up our dreams to make room for miracles. We have to gather up the deadness and start a bonfire. Let the ashes paint the canvas of our lives. The sorrow has a place and it will never leave, even if miracles come, and that's okay. We have to stay alert. Watching. Listening. Keeping our eyes peeled for the miracle.

And I'll tell you what the miracle will be. I know already. *The miracle will be the redemption of our pain.*

In the book of Genesis we read the story of Joseph. Rejected and cast away by his brothers, made a slave, then a prisoner, and finally ruler of Egypt. His life, in many ways, was filled with brokenness. At one point he says to his brothers, *you meant evil against me, but God meant it for good…* (Genesis 15:20 NASB)

He had found the miracle. The redemption of his pain. The purpose, just as the blind man found, in his "years of darkness." But it did not mean that the pain went away. For better or worse, Joseph had to live until the day he died with the fact that his brothers rejected him.

It is the same in the story of Job. He lost his money, his livelihood, his health, and all of his children. There are chapters and chapters in the Bible about Job coming to the end of himself—giving glory to God in his pain but also struggling with horrible depression and hopelessness.

At the end of his story we hear him say, "My ears had heard of you but now my eyes have seen you." (42:5) In the middle of his pain, he saw God. As he acknowledges the Lord's place in his life, he is given back all of his wealth plus more, his health, and he has ten more children. *He was given a miracle, the redemption of his pain.*

But there is still sorrow in miracles. Job was given ten more children but I guarantee you that he mourned the ones he lost until the day he died. The birth of new children never takes away the loss of ones buried.

For my husband, the miracle, the redemption, came in the form of a fourteen-year-old boy who started coming to the farm to work. He started calling us *Ma* and *Pa* and learned how to fix tractors and plant fields at my husband's side. A boy that we simply would not have had time for if we had the children we desired.

We were blessed with a surrogate-son only because, for this period of our lives, we have burned the dream of our own children. God took the ashes and created beauty because that's what He does.

I, too, have caught glimpses of my pain being redeemed. During the week, I get to pour my "mother-heart" onto two little boys. Boys who give me sticky-snotty kisses and catch frogs for me from the creek. Boys who give me Mother's Day cards and say, "You're the best part-time mom ever!"

Does it change the fact that I mourn not having my own babies? Of course not! But when I am given the chance to tell the gospel story to a five-year-old who is listening with wide-eyes as we bake cookies, I witness a miracle, the redemption of my pain.

It was during a visit to Haiti, two years after we lived there, that I finally began recognizing the miracle of redemption.

"Pain Redeemed"

The laundry was just dry enough not to drip, the best that the tiny, ill-behaved washer could do. I snapped the shirt roughly, trying to shake off any excess water. Even in the eighty-degree weather, it would take all day to dry. The line dipped under the weight.

The men's voices from the porch drifted across the yard. It still felt so strange, this understanding a foreign language. What used to sound like background noise now formed words that then formed thoughts. My husband was telling a group of men the gospel story.

As the last piece of laundry was placed over the line a statement from one of the men made me turn my head, "If God cares about me then why can't I find work to provide for my family?"

In Haiti the unemployment rate is over forty percent and two-thirds of the "employed" people do not have formal jobs. It's a big deal. It's hard, much harder than we Americans can even understand. I watched my husband's face. How would he respond? What response was there?

"Do you think God cares about me because I have work and money?" He asked the question gently and the men chorused affirmation. In their eyes it was simple: God loved us because He made us Americans. We got opportunity. We got money. We got white skin. End of story.

"So, if God cares about me," he continued, "then why can't my wife have babies?"

The question stunned them into silence. In their culture, having children sits on the same level as having money. The men, now lacking words of argument, listened as he went on, "I'm not saying that God doesn't care about me. He does. But I don't get all the things that I want, even if I'm American. God's favor is not based on worldly things. Not money. Not babies. Not nationality. Nothing here…"

Their conversation drifted out of earshot and I went inside to prepare rice and beans for lunch. My husband came through a few minutes later to get his Bible. He came over to me with it in his hands, "Tash, do you mind if I give this away?" The second year of our marriage, I had scrimped and saved to buy him a leather-bound Bible for his birthday, "One of the guys can read English but he doesn't have a Bible."

"Of course you have to give it to him," I said. Our eyes met for just a moment and I hoped, prayed, that the pride I felt for him showed. Because it is so amazingly wonderful to know that God is using your husband. Speaking and touching lives through him. And nothing is more wonderful than knowing that God is working to redeem your pain.

It's the story He's been teaching me. The story of redemption. It's the story of Jesus and it's His story for me.

God may someday give us a miracle, maybe more than one! But there is sorrow, even in miracles. Nothing, no matter what it is, will take away the sorrow of my years without babies.

But even one more soul in heaven is worth a lifetime without children.

And that is something I believe with all my heart.

While living in Haiti we would often have groups come to visit and work for a few weeks. In late July, Cole and Jan, a couple who had been struggling with infertility for over ten years, brought a group down that consisted of several students from the public school where Jan taught.

One of the young girls went for a walk with me and as we talked I found a glimpse into the miraculous beauty of a God who paints masterpieces out of ashes.

"I don't understand why Jan isn't a mom," she told me, "she would be the best mom in the world. There are so many children that end up in terrible homes; I can't fathom why God wouldn't allow Jan to be the mother of at least one of them."

We continued walking, our skin prickling with moisture in the humidity. We were just passing the banana tree, almost to the bridge that went over the creek, when she said the words. They came out in almost a whisper, "Of course, I feel guilty even saying this, but I'm thankful that Jan hasn't had children yet. If she did, I know that she wouldn't be working, and having her for a teacher has changed my life. I know God because Jan's dreams didn't come true." She looked over at me, "I want her to have a baby so badly but I also can't imagine not knowing Him."

Jan's story is layered with ashes. Ten years. Ten years of banging her head against closed doors. Ten years of watching other women bear and raise the babies she ached for.

Ten years of saying—*Why, God? What am I not doing right? What am I doing wrong? How can I make You pleased enough with me to give me a child?*

She experienced failed procedures, a molar pregnancy, hormonal imbalance, millions of tears and sorrows so deep they left wounds on her heart.

The change came when she fell to her knees and said, "Lord, I'm tired of slamming against closed doors. You show us what to do. You show us where to go. If You open the door, we'll walk through."

The next morning their pastor showed up, stepped into their kitchen, and said, "What do you think about working with the youth group?"

A wide-open door.

Trembling, they walked through. And God redeemed their pain.

Lives have been transformed; young people are following Christ, lights shimmering in darkness. All because this beautiful woman offered what she had to a God who performs miracles.

A miracle is the redemption of pain, not the absolution of it. The years that Jan spent longing and hoping for a child are not absolved by the fact that she was able to lead other young people into a closer walk with God.

But there is a taste of redemption. A little glimpse into the eternal purpose. Like Jesus saying, as He did with the blind man, *this happened so that the work of God may be displayed...* It is a reminder of what God is creating out of our ashes.

Every miracle contains sorrow, for without pain there is no need for a miracle. But they also contain redemption. The kind that is so full of light and beauty that it hurts to look at them.

Jan's story didn't end there. Less than a year after their visit to Haiti, she and her husband were asked if they would be willing to adopt a baby girl. She became a mom, just like she dreamed. But here is the catch: she still mourns the children she never had.

The idea that *if our dreams come true, we'll be free from pain* is a lie. The idea that *if we give up our dreams, we'll always be empty* is also a lie.

Only in emptiness can we be filled. Only in the burning of our dreams can we glimpse the redemption that God offers.

Beauty For Ashes

He offers beauty for ashes
Strength for our pain
Hope for all who call on His name.
He offers to hold all our tears
Clothe us in white
And turn the dark into light.

But so often we forget…
To get beauty for ashes, something must burn
To get strength for pain, something must hurt
For Him to hold all our tears, we must cry
To turn the dark into light, we have to face a black night

All His promises are true
He'll do just what He said He'd do.
Yet so many times,
In the fire, pain and tears
We hide in the darkness
And cry out in fear
"Where are you, God?
Where are you, God?"

And He says,
"To get beauty for ashes, something must burn
To get strength for pain, something must hurt
For Me to hold all your tears, you must cry
To turn the dark into light, you have to face a black night

But I promise you,
In the end,
I will make all things new."

Personal Study Guide

1. I shared that even if our dreams came true, we would still not be free from pain. What dreams have you had that you thought would save you from the pain you've experienced? What have you believed about God's love for you because of how those dreams have lived or died? How have these beliefs held up when compared with the Bible?

2. What dreams or hopes have died that you still need to mourn? Are there feelings of anger, bitterness, or fear that you have stuffed inside? Our God is a gentle God, who knows our tears. Read Psalm 42, and allow the Comforter to draw near to you.

3. In this chapter, my husband has a conversation with some Haitian men about what God's favor is not. What do you believe God's favor looks like? Explore this further by reading Psalm 41:11, Ephesians 1:3, Genesis 4:3-5, Genesis 6:7-9, Esther 2:8-9, Psalm 30:6-7, Isaiah 66:2b, and 2 Corinthians 6:2.

4. Have you been embracing that idea that God's path, though not the one you would have chosen, is the best one for you, and for the world? Or have you been fighting this way? Read Isaiah 55, and note verses 8-9. Ask the Lord to give you a vision for what his plan in your life looks like, and to give you a joy for the dreams he has for you, and to give you strength to let the dreams die that keep you from his way.

Chapter Eight

"Circumstances change but Truth does not."
-journal entry

Tim and Rhonda battled infertility for years. She felt the isolation that comes when all your friends have baby after baby and you have none. Treatments, desperate prayers, dying hope…

In her words, *The Biblical word [for infertility] is barrenness and I found it to be a very appropriate word. Infertility is a dry, brittle, lonely, unproductive wasteland. It is hard to find any good in a barren landscape. Friendships dry up. Stacks of disappointing months add up to irreplaceable years. Hopes are vaporous mirages, ever on the horizon but never producing reality. Prayers are whittled down to desperate pleas for that out-of-reach hope-denied. Infertility is a major, life-altering, on-going desert.*

There were moments of oasis in this desert.

One Sunday morning, half-way through their journey, their announcement of a coming child traveled through church and people were laughing, crying, jumping over pews, rushing to the front to rejoice with them.

And here is the glory—she bore a son.

And here is the pain—he was the only child she would ever give birth to.

An oasis in the desert is beautiful, but they are few and far between. There may be a time to rejoice and drink the life-giving water, but those who think, "If I could just have this one thing I desire, I would be content," well, that's not really how it works.

Contentment is not found in the fulfillment of desire, or the lack of desire. It is only found in the surrendering of desire.

Surrender is the only path to freedom. I must allow God to rule without trying to dictate His hand. I must recognize that getting what I want will never set me free.

For Rhonda, the birth of her son was glorious, a miracle. Yet, it was not the end of her desire for children. She still journeyed through rough seas and crashing waves. She still faced storms that left her battered. She still had dreams that continued to die.

She had to make a choice, somewhere out there in the middle of the pain, if she was going to surrender to a God that she did not understand.

She says, *The spiritual crisis that infertility created in my life dried up the reserves I had to be "good" on my own. I was already a Christian but I truly encountered my ongoing need for a Savior on a whole new level. I had to contemplate that some of the mysteries of God would forever be beyond my grasp to explain or understand and that was okay— because He was God and I was not.*

Job, in the depths of his pain, says, *If only my anguish could be weighed and all my misery be placed on the scales! It would surely outweigh the sands of the sea...* (6:2)

He cries, trembles in horror at the ashes of his life, and then God speaks. *Then the Lord answered Job out of the storm.* (38:1) And I am struck by the fact that it is a storm, a wild, billowing storm that He speaks from. His voice thunders. The foundations of the earth quake.

And I'm bowed low in humbleness.

We cannot forget who we are speaking to when we demand answers from God. We are free to be real, to be hurting, and to be lost and angry. Yet, in the end—He is God and we are not.

Another dear friend told me the story of her journey through infertility. She sat in the doctor's office after another failed procedure and the nurse said, "We can get you a baby."

Something clicked.

"No one," she told me, "can give life but God Himself, and I needed to recognize that I am nothing and He is everything. If He chooses to keep me from having children, I need to surrender."

She was humbled. Forced to look at her inability to change her circumstances.

And here is the beauty—she has been transformed.

God became real. Breath on your face, voice in your ear, hand in your hand—real.

In the surrender, in the emptying of self, in the acknowledgment of God, we find the contentment our souls desire. We find the face of God.

The physical desire may never leave.

I want a baby.

I may very well want a baby until the day I die.

I don't have to try and convince myself to not want children. Contentment is not the absence of desire. But my ability to live with joy between here and death is dependent not on the fulfillment of my desires but on the surrender of them. It's not easy. It may look like simple words on paper when I type, *If it be your will, Lord, I am willing to go through this life without a child.* But there is agony mingled with the lines and curves of those letters.

Rhonda and Jan both tasted the fulfillment of their desires, they became mothers. Yet, they say the same thing: *The desire for children doesn't go away, even with a baby.*

Jan told me, "It comes back to me and God. Back to me not being in charge. Some days I hate that I can't control my life—but every day I am thankful that God allowed me to walk through the thing that would make me know Him for real."

Her surrender, her acknowledgment of God's position, her humbleness—those things burst open doors for Jesus Christ to live through her. She has found contentment in surrender.

It was just after the roller coaster ride through the storms of adoption, when they finally were holding a baby girl in their arms, that Jan realized the depths of her transformation. She sat in the living room feeding her new daughter and found herself praying, *Oh, Lord, don't let having a child make me lose the closeness I've found with you.*

Having an overwhelmingly deep relationship with the Redeemer Himself will trump every other miracle.

Personal Study Guide

1. "Circumstances change, but Truth does not." The truth is: you were created for an intimate relationship with Christ, and the circumstances in your life can either push you closer to Him or farther away. And which they do is entirely up to you. How have you allowed the circumstances of your life to push or pull you away from the Savior? How can you plan for the future to remember which direction to go?

2. Barren. Webster's defines it as "not reproducing, devoid, lacking, lacking interest or charm, or lacking inspiration or ideas." What other talents, hopes, and dreams in your life have been overtaken by barrenness because of the sorrow you have been experiencing? How has the world been lacking because of those things? How can you allow the Lord to fill you with inspiration, ideas, and interest again?

3. I mentioned the relationship between surrender and contentment. Do you find yourself struggling with discontentment? What things do you want that you are convinced would satisfy you? What are you afraid of if you surrender these things?

4. At the end of the book of Job, he says, "My ears had heard of you but now my eyes have seen you." What if his way is pain, sorrow, and the death of every dream you've held? Is knowing Him still worth it to you? Can you read Philippians 3:7-11 and agree with every word? Ask the Lord to show you what you're still clinging to besides the hope of finding the face of God.

Chapter Nine

Love the Lord your God...
-Mark 12:30

When struggling with difficult concepts I often try to break them down into parable form. The simplicity of a short story can often ease my mind into understanding the real issue. This parable came to me while contemplating the arrival of Mother's Day and the difficulties that holiday brings to those of us battling infertility. These same truths can be applied to any issue you may currently be dealing with.

No matter our struggles, no matter our pain, no matter our fears—we are all asked the same question.

The Parable of the Silver Locket

She dreamed of it from the time she was a little girl. Some day beyond the tomorrows she would be big enough to have her own. *A beautiful silver locket.*

Some girls scoffed at the idea of a locket. They didn't want one. They didn't need one. Many received them anyway.

Some girls threw theirs away.

Some girls had so many they nearly crawled under the weight of their treasures.

Some girls treated them with disdain. Leaving them, neglecting them, allowing them to be tarnished and misused.

It seemed that they were everywhere so the girl never thought that when she was old enough there would be no locket for her.

None.

Not even a little one.

Not even a broken one.

Nothing for the girl with the dream.

She searched for discarded ones. Perhaps she could dig one out of the dirt and restore it? She didn't need a new one. A used one would do.

One time she found a newly created one, tiny and precious, about to be thrown away. Maybe, maybe this one would be hers? But the other-girl rose in fury, "It's mine," she insisted.

"But you don't want it," the girl pointed out, hope brimming.

The other-girl just scoffed, "It's still mine." She proceeded to crush the locket to pieces, silver dust forever lost, blown in the wind.

In desperation the girl went to the only place she knew. Down in the very center of town, where the Locket-Maker worked and lived.

She knocked at the door and let it creak slowly open when she heard the deep voice answer.

He was there. Tall and dark and warm. A comfortableness filtered out of him and freed the tears that had been threatening to fall. The girl stood for some time in the doorway, taking deep breaths and wiping away the droplets of salt-water that stained her cheeks.

The Locket-Maker stepped closer, "What do you need, dear one?" he asked.

"P-p-please, kind sir," she whispered, "may I please have a locket?"

"There are many lockets in the world," he said.

"I know," her voice strengthened, "but I have longed for one of my own. Please, I would treasure it always."

The Locket-Maker looked at her carefully. "Come," he said, offering his hand. He led her outside and together they looked over the town surrounding them. "I know your heart," he finally answered, "I have watched you learn to care for and protect my lockets. This is good. You can help others."

"But, Mr. Locket-Maker," she explained, "many won't listen to me. They don't believe that I know how because I don't have my own. If I could just have one, even a used one or a lost one or a tarnished one, anything, then I'll help others. I just," she paused and motioned with her arms, "I just long for something so precious, so valuable, something to give me purpose."

The Locket-Maker looked at her thoughtfully. "Does it have to be yours to be precious? Do you have to possess it to offer it value? Can you, will you, be willing to polish and protect others lockets simply because I made them?"

The questions made her heart shake. She knew that he could just make her one. It wasn't hard. He had the supplies.

She knew him well. She had spent days in his workshop. They talked often and shared deep secrets. Why would he ask something like this of her? Why let her heart long for something he could provide? Why ask her to serve the very ones who were neglecting the gift she dreamed of?

She wanted to cry. To beg. To plead. But when she looked up into his eyes, something stopped her. More questions, this time unspoken but echoing, filled her mind.

Was it possible to love the created more than the Creator? Did she love him for who he was not just for what he could give? If he tore away her dreams, would she still remain his?

Then the questions seemed to change their form. They melted together and one burning inquiry remained. *Do you love me?*

She fell to her knees outside his workshop. Had she loved him just for what he could give her? The question mattered little now. The only thing that remained was her answer. *Did she love him?*

"I do," she whispered, "I do."

Through the seasons that followed she saw that everything the Locket-Maker did was to ask the deep-deep question of all hearts, *"Do you love me?"*

To some he gave lockets and lockets and lockets and the weight of their care brought them to his door.

Others received lockets only for a short time and when they shattered and were gone they came crawling to his feet.

Others received no locket at all.

But the choice for all was the same—live in emptiness or grace. Love the Locket-Maker for who he was and not for what he gave—or turn their hearts away.

And the girl began to see a glimpse of something that ran deep and long. She was the Locket-Maker's treasured possession. What he wanted, the thing he desired, was her heart.

Personal Study Guide

1. What would you ask the Locket Maker if you could sit at his table? What do you think he would ask you?

2. In Psalms, Hosea, and the Gospels, it says over and over again that the Lord speaks through parables. Ask the Lord to show you a parable from your own life that reveals your journey. Write it out, and ask Him to show you someone he'd like to encourage with it.

3. The question is asked again and again, "Do you love Him?" Let that question sink down into your heart. Let the Lord reveal your true-heart, and where you've withheld it from your Maker.

Chapter Ten

Hope that is seen is no hope at all.
-Romans 8:24

As the five-year mark of trying to conceive grew closer, the inner places in me started withering. I had said that I would carry the burden of childlessness, as long as He carried me, but parts of me never quite believed that I would have to. I could see purpose in the past but was shivering in fear over the future.

I can tell you right now what comes with hopelessness—depression. It skimmed the edges of my mind, attacked when I looked in the mirror, laughed in glee when I stared at my unchanging temperature morning after morning. It was there, and I was losing the fight, again.

I never knew what would send depression spiraling. It just appeared and I was lost.

A friend pointing out that I couldn't understand the bond between a mother and child hurt so desperately. She didn't mean to wound me, I know, but the words left me crushed and bleeding.

Visiting an antique shop and finding a treasure trove of little girl wonders. Pointing them out to my husband and saying, "If we had a little girl…" My voice trailing off and my heart dipping into sadness.

Slow steps toward adoption and then something pushes the timetable back, *way back*. And I crumble.

No warnings. No, "prepare yourself." Nothing. Just heartache.

Battles I thought were done and gone lifting to the surface, exploding sorrow, and making me want to hide.

I believed with all my heart that God, in His love and mercy, had a plan for me. But that doesn't mean I didn't long for something different.

It was late one evening when I faced my growing panic. My husband was gone for the night and I sat at the table with my Bible open before me. "Okay, God," I said, "show me what to do with this."

His voice said only one word in reply.

Love.

It wasn't a reason. It was a command. I was to love, deeply and fully. To reach out and out and out.

When depression reared its ugly head, my retaliation was love. It was when I stopped giving, when I stopped reaching out, when my gaze fell back onto myself, that depression and hopelessness rang victorious in my life.

Matchless Grace

The morning sun rises
Soft and slow upon the eastern sky
Another day has come and my heart whispers
"Why?"
I want more than anything
To hide my face again
But God in His patience
Love and firmness
Pulls me from my self-consumed
Depression
To say…

Why are you hiding, O, Daughter of mine?
Why are you wishing
To escape this life?
I created you to face what is before
To walk, not alone, but with me guiding
To be a witness
Not of perfection
But of my infinite, matchless
Grace.

The cure for the depression that plagued me was love. Not to love myself more, but to love others with the deep, overflowing, triumphing love of the Savior.

The One who walked through pain *on purpose* so that He might give more.

As much as infertility has caused me pain, I can truly say that I am better for it. I've learned more, seen more. I have felt the touch of the Father and tasted the flavoring of grace that is only found through heartache. I have been knocked flat, forced to look at Him with true eyes.

He is. And I am not.

There are days that I try to be god in my life. I fight and scratch my way to the top, only to find that I've been burying myself deeper in selfish pride. Pulling myself away from grace.

There is a reason I am writing this book today and not tomorrow. Dear ones, *I am still here.* I still have the dirt under my fingernails and the tears are still staining my cheeks and there are still days when my heartbreak leaves bloody trails behind me.

And yet, I have overcome.

I say this with fear and trembling but I say it. I have overcome infertility even though I still struggle with it.

The concept still throws me. How does one overcome something they are still fighting? But is this not, again, where my human mentality clashes head-on with God's way of thinking? I only see today and no further. God sees long-term. The depths of my heart in all eternity.

He is well aware that I am sin-based. He is well aware that I will continually struggle with the surrendering of my desires. And still He calls me to be an overcomer.

It cannot be that overcoming means the end of struggles. He says, *In this world you will have trouble.* (John 16:33)

That verse has been in my vocabulary for most of my life but I didn't apply it long-term. In fact, I like to take all His statements lightly. Sure, there will be trouble. There are car accidents, animals die, bad things happen.

No, no. This statement is coming from a man who will be beaten, broken, rejected, ignored, abandoned, and killed. It is spoken to a world where there are car accidents that tear off limbs and people waste away with diseases. Missionaries offer love and are slaughtered, girls dive into lakes and break their necks, dreams are shattered, babies are stillborn, marriages crumble, children rebel. Life creaks and groans and slices us wide open with unbearable pain—again and again and again.

In this world you will have trouble. But take heart! I have overcome the world. (John 16:33)

He has overcome my problems, my pain, and my heartache—whatever sorrows that stomp through my life. And here is the key, the shuddering truth that makes my fingers tremble as I type:

I can overcome, even as I struggle. I have been crucified with Christ and no longer live, instead He now lives in me and He has overcome the world.

I just have to remember. I have to keep my stubborn, sinful heart in a state of humbleness. The moment I forget, the moment I let my clawing for self-righteousness triumph, I pull myself off the altar. I take back my life and find that all I gain is death.

The only way to overcome is recognize that I am going to die, one way or another. I will die with agony in my sins or die with joy in Him.

I choose Him.

I will continue to choose Him.

Psalm 107 says,

> *He brought them out of*
> *darkness and deepest gloom*
> *and broke away their chains.*
> *Let them give thanks to the Lord*
> *for his unfailing love... (14-15)*

I wish it stopped there but it doesn't.

> *Some became fools through*
> *their rebellious ways,*
> *and suffered affliction*
> *because of their iniquities...(17)*

This is pretty much my story.

I fought God for so long. I wanted to be in charge. And me being in charge would mean no pain. But that's not how it works. That was my rebellious nature wanting to be god. Wasn't that what got the human race in trouble in the first place?

But thankfully, it doesn't stop there either.

> *Then they cried to the Lord in their trouble,*
> *and he saved them from their distress;*
> *He sent forth his word and healed them;*
> *He rescued them from the grave.*
> *Let them give thanks to the Lord*
> *for his unfailing love...*
> *Let them sacrifice thank offerings*
> *and tell of his works with songs of joy. (20-22)*

Natasha Metzler

So hands raised, I sing. And I will keep singing. I will keep striving. I will keep laying down the idol of "self." I'll keep falling at the feet of the One who saves and heals and brings songs of joy to those who are hurting.

The One who takes broken, bitter hearts and makes them sweet.

The God I serve parted the Red Sea thousands of years ago and continues to part the obstacles in my life. *He's a miracle worker.*

He met three men in a blazing furnace and continues to meet me right in the midst of my fiery trials. *He's not afraid of pain and will stand with me in it.*

He defeated a giant and continues to slay the giants in my life. *There is nothing on this earth too difficult for Him.*

He shut the mouths of lions and He will also shut down the Enemy who is seeking to devour me. *He is my champion.*

He's a God of miracles. A God of redemption.

I can just barely hear His whisper at times but it is there, rising on the wings of the dawn. I don't believe for a second that my infertility was a surprise to God. I don't believe it was a mistake. So I'm going to use it.

Instead of allowing infertility to control me, I'm going to give that right into God's hands. Even if I have to force myself onto my knees every day, humble myself before a mighty God, and say, "Use everything, even my pain, to bring You glory."

Because it's not about me. It was never about me. It's about Him.

Personal Study Guide

1. Read Romans 8, and note the words "desire," "suffering," "hope," and "wait." How does this compare to what you're experiencing? Now read it again, and look for what God desires, how He has suffered, what he hopes for, and what he's waiting for.

2. In the beginning of this chapter, I mention that new battles arise often without warning. The war is not over, even if we have the tools and means to win. How can you prepare yourself for upcoming battles? How can you keep truth constantly in your mind, before your eyes, so that when the enemy attacks, you are on your guard and ready to run to the Lord, not away from him?

3. I shared that the Lord's answer to my depression was to reach out to others in love. Have you done this, or has your sorrow caused you to retreat, or to be mostly a "taker" and rarely a "giver?" Ask the Lord to open your eyes to see what he sees in your life.

4. You are called to be an overcomer. You will continually struggle, you will still have to fight, you will have trouble, but He has overcome the world, and he has called you to Victory. Read 2 Corinthians 2:14-16. What example do you give to the world around you of the power that we have through Christ? Have your words and testimony compelled others to seek the hope you have?

5. Read Psalm 107. Consider the list of those redeemed by the Lord. Can you write your own psalm of how you were rescued, delivered, and blessed? Lift your hands in praise and "thank the LORD for his steadfast love, for his wondrous works to the children of man!"

6. The idea of *Pain Redeemed* is the idea that our good and loving God has a plan for redemption, a plan that doesn't make light of your pain or ignore it, but a plan that actually uses your pain to bring beauty and good into your life, and into the world. This is only possible by you submitting your heart and saying "Use everything, even my pain, to bring You glory." If you are willing, take a minute on your knees to do this, and let the Lord minister to you and give you a hope of the beautiful things to come.

Epilogue

Writing this book has not been easy for me. I can string together fictional stories and I can produce a well-placed blog post but a book about me is stretching my abilities. I have so many questions. How much of my story do I tell? How can I be faithful with the stories that have been shared with me?

Every person who reads this book comes from a different place. A different pain. A different heartache. You know different things about God and have different predisposed world-views.

As I write I feel compelled to ask: what, friend, is your pain? What wounds and fires have defined you? I walked into my story with a level of knowledge about God and redemption and deep, deep love. *What about you?*

What do you know about God? Have you seen Him? Have you heard Him? Has He transformed you? Have you walked through sin and bitterness into humble confession? The glory of redemption?

In Isaiah 59 the story of His redemption is unveiled. The first half speaks of sin and iniquities, of blood-guilt and lies, of greed and death. And then God looks.

"He saw that there was no one, he was appalled that there was no one to intervene; so his own arm worked salvation for him and his own righteousness sustained him." (16)

And Jesus is there, hundreds of years before His birth, His heart breaking to free the lost. And He does. He lives, breathes, dies—to offer us redemption from our sins and from our pain.

Not the absolution of our sins and pain, not yet. It will be, in the end. But today, in this moment, we are given redemption.

When I die to myself, when I pour out my life to Him, accepting the road that He has given me to walk (with all its sorrow) He redeems.

Depression doesn't stand a chance in the face of hope.

Hope in a God whose love is not measured by fulfilled dreams. His love *is.* It matters not what I have or do not have.

Hope in a God who tears down the walls that keep me from a real relationship with Him—even if the tearing down wounds me.

And here it is. The promise that makes my heart beat wild with joy. *He wounds in order to heal and every taste of sorrow will be redeemed in time.*

About the Author

Natasha Metzler lives with her husband on a dairy farm in Northern New York. She is continuing to learn how to embrace the miracle of serving a God who redeems. You can find her blogging at natashametzler.com

She loves to hear from her readers and can be reached by emailing, natashametzler@gmail.com

Bonus Material

Dying of Thirst at the Side of a Well
A MANIFESTO

> # Infertility painted my life black.

At the diagnosis, dreams died
slow agonizing deaths.
Hope for the future crumbled
and tears left muddied smears on my soul.
Every part of me hurt.

This was my greatest desire,
what I felt
in my bones
I was created to do.

Mama was the title I wanted most, yet could not attain.

So I cried in agony,
and lost myself in the blackness of night.

Darkness ruled.

It stole time,
sneaking in and rearranging life,
leaving me to stumble in the blackness--
wounding myself on relationships and fears.

I ached,
and I did not know why.

With the ground moving under me,
and my greatest desires yanked from my grasp,
I was lost.

Then life stilled in one quiet moment.

My hands gripping the kitchen table, my heart
clenching in understanding,
depression was named and I breathed deep.

Pain Redeemed

My mother sat with me that day, speaking truth
into the lies that had wrapped their webs around
my heart. She did not flinch at my ugly hurts. She
did not hide from my pain. She sat strong and
spoke true and her words were a light that
splintered through my blackness.

This wasn't real.
It was an enemy sent to suck my life away,
but with the naming it lost its power.

I gathered forces to fight the darkness and
embrace the light.

> Ask and it will be
> given to you;
> seek and you will find;
> knock and the door
> will be opened to you.
> (Matthew 7:7)

Scripture verses painted my vision and I reached with desperate fingers to catch the hope of escape.

Ask.

> So I asked,
>> I begged,
>>> I cried.

Seek.

> I searched,
>> tore open,
>>> sought.

Knock.

> I pounded on the door of heaven
> until my hands were raw and bleeding.

And silence echoed.

> I cried in fury and agony.
> I writhed in the pain of
> betrayal.

After all the fighting and crawling to reach for light, I heard only silence as the darkness closed back over me. I had believed and hoped and dreamed and yet, still, I was left to wallow in anger and fear.

"God!" my voice screamed to the heavens,

"Where are you?
How can you, *my loving God*, be silent
while my heart is slain?"

I could not endure without relief,
I could not continue to live this life of agony.

"Either take this pain away by giving me the child
I so desperately need,
or take away the need,

but, dear God,
by God!
do not leave me here."

The silence that followed shook the foundations
of my faith.

"There must be a key,"
my heart whispered.

My shaking hands tore open the Scripture,
my desperate heart clawed through the pages--
A key,
any key,
to move the hand of God.

How did Hannah, Sarah, and Rachel convince God
to move on their behalf? What did the mother of
Samson do to bring the angel of the Lord to her
side?

Perhaps I could find the answer if I searched.

Genesis, Exodus, Leviticus, Numbers...
Isaiah, Jeremiah, Lamentations, Ezekiel...
Haggai, Zechariah, Malachi, Matthew...

The books passed under my eyes,
and blindness healed.
I dropped to my knees,
and cried.

> I was in a desert.
> A vast, empty,
> no-drop-of-life-in-sight
> desert.

As far as I could see, this desert of infertility reigned. It stretched out in every direction with only a path marked through the middle to show the way. A path surrounded on every side by deadness and fear.

And I stood,
      dehydrated,
            starving,
                  covered in sand and dust,
screaming at the heavens,

"God, I cannot walk this road!"

Natasha Metzler

My fists shook,
and my knees quaked
as death and darkness stalked me.
My heart so full of fear
it left an acrid taste upon my tongue.

Blind eyes blazing,
deaf ears roaring,
my voice hoarse from tears,
I broke.

> # Scripture washed the scales from my eyes.

As I clawed through the pages, my parched heart searching for truth,
the Words trickled down.

Bubbling and **splashing**, they grew in my conscience until I realized that they had always been there, even when I thought there was only silence.

They were lapping against the edges of my understanding--

"My daughter,"
  this voice whispered, spoke, shouted,
   "You have to walk this road,
    But I will walk it with you."

There was no escaping, no jumping the desert.
There was no forgetting the desire, pretending it
had never existed.
There was only the long, long road--
as far as the eye could see--
of desert wanderings.

My choices were simple: walk this road or stand
with my fist raised to the heavens. But either
way, the desert was here to stay.

"I will die," I finally broke,
"I am dying of thirst already.
I will starve.
I'll waste away before
I find hope."

Gently, softly, He continued speaking.
Roaring, crashing, the words flowed over me,
again and again and again.

I AM with you. I AM with you. I AM with you.

O God, O God.
It dawns as the wave washes over me.

I'm dying of thirst
at the side of a well;

I'm dying of thirst beside the Living Water.

"Eat of my body,
drink of my
Spirit," He says.

(in John 6:54)

The desert path that I must walk
continues as far as the eye can see.

I have to journey through it, however long it lasts,
but I am not left alone.
I was never alone.

His Spirit fills and quenches thirst
in a way that the objects of my desire
never could.

I am given water in the desert
from the Rock of Ages.
I am given food,
the Bread of His Word.

Pain Redeemed

Manna.
New every morning.
I can turn and drink deep,
I can open the Word and eat my fill.

I am dying of thirst only when I have turned my
back on Him.

I am starving only when I refuse to gain my
sustenance from what He has already given.

> I walk this road,
> but not alone.

He is with me.

The road may end tomorrow,
next year,
ten years from now.
Perhaps it will continue for the rest of my life.

But He is with me.

The desert is still full of agony,
of loss,
of shaking sorrows,

but I can walk on day after day after day,
because even though I have nothing--

He is.
Water. *Bread.* Life.

"One thing I do know.
I was blind but now I see!"
-John 9:25

Pain Redeemed

Made in the USA
Lexington, KY
26 February 2014